Mr. Saved's W.O.W

Words   **Of**   **Wisdom**

Presents

TRUE FRIENDS

MICHAEL ROSE

Copyright © 2016 by Michael Rose
Long Beach, California

All Rights Reserved
Printed and Bound in the United States of America

Wisdom Says Publishing House
Long Beach, California
Email: mrsaved5007@gmail.com

Cover Design/Illustrations: Jay De Vance Herndon
Formatting: TWA Solutions
First Printing, March 2016
10 9 8 7 6 5 4 3 2 1
ISBN: 978-0-692-25012-9

Publisher's Note
All rights reserved. No part of this book may be reproduced in whole or in part, in any form or by any means, electronic or mechanical, including photocopying, recording or by any information storage and retrieval system, without permission in writing from the author.

Acknowledgments

This book is dedicated to my God, who has always been there for me, to my grandfather, L.B. Rose, and to so many other people, good and bad, who inspired me to write this book. Thank you for helping me reach my level.

True Friends,
They'll tell you the truth when no one will,
But, always, of course, in love.
They'll be that swift kick in the pants
That's harmless like a dove.

At times, you two will stand opposed,
At times, you two will clash,
But, even the moments of dispute
Will never seem to last.

They'll be right there to applaud all your success and fame,
And they'll celebrate you. They'll let you shine;
They'll be your picture frame.

And, if they have no money to lend,
They'll say, "Hold on; I'll phone a friend."
They won't just leave you high and dry,
As if your need has passed you by.
They'll do their very best for you.
They won't just leave you there to stew.
They'll do their best to rescue you.
For, this is what true friends do.

And it doesn't matter what time it is,
How busy they are or how hard it's been,
They'll take the time to help you out,
Even if they, too, are facing a drought,
Even if they, too, can't figure things out
Because the two of you can "stick-it-out,"
When life becomes a ruthless bout.

And if you both reach the ends of your ropes,
After trying every single approach,
Then the two of you will make a toast,
To suffer together, at the most.

And if the landlord kicks you out,
And you need to sleep on your friend's couch,
Even if they have a bitter spouse,
They'll never ask out the side of their mouth,
And they'll never ask with an empty heart,
Then tell you, "Well, I did my part."

And if they say, "No," then they'll "Flip out."
They'll show them what it's all about;
They'll flip a chair, throw a shoe, break a lamp, blow a fuse,
And they'll do this all in front of you,
Just to let you know they're true.
And when you go to tie your shoe,
They'll say, "Wait up! I'm coming, too!"

For, this is what true friends do.

And when you're stuck in a rut, they'll pick you up,
They'll motivate you; they'll fill your cup.
They'll bring the fun when you're undone.
Whenever, you're feeling bottom-rung.
And they'll make you laugh, and they'll make you run.
When all you can do is sit and hum.

You see, they'll be another part of you,
When you can't seem to make it through,
And they'll sit right there, with eyes on you.
For this is what true friends do.

And when a threat presents itself,
They will bear their teeth
Like a lion, true and strong. They will never flee.
They'll ready their sword and shield for battle
Against the one who dares,
And they'll stand with you, side by side,
Even if they're scared.

And together, you'll fight, lose or win,
Because a problem with you, is a problem with them.

And when life gets hot, they'll be your shade,
They'll be your glass of lemonade.
They'll be a spring, cool and deep,
The softest chair to rest your feet,
And the biggest umbrella on the beach.

They'll be your tree that blocks the rays,
And you'll hide there until the heat wave fades.

You see,
They'll give it their all because that's what friends do,
But, even more so, when they're true.
And every day, they'll prove it to you,
And you'll prove it to them,
You'll do this, too.
For, this is what true friends do.

www.ingramcontent.com/pod-product-compliance
Lightning Source LLC
Chambersburg PA
CBRC092342290426
44110CB00008B/186